Birds

Children's Nature Library

PUBLICATIONS INTERNATIONAL, LTD.

8 7 6 5 4 3 2 1

ISBN 0-88176-626-7

Contributing Author: Teri Crawford Jones

Credits:
Animals/Animals: Henry Ausloos: 14; Hans & Judy Beste: 44, 62; Patricia Caulfield: 48; M.A. Chappell: 51; John Chellman: 17, 35; Ken Cole: 59; Margot Conte: 26; Bruce Davidson: 8; Michael Dick: 14, 16, 28, 62; Michael Fogden: 10, 16; Arthur Gloor: 42; Marcia W. Griffen: 10, 11; William D. Griffen: 56; Johnny Johnson: 31; Breck P. Kent: 61; Richard Kolar: 13; Zig Leszczynski: 7, 8, 36; Robert A. Lubeck: 44, Back Cover; Joe McDonald: 34; Stefan Meyers: 27; Patti Murray: 44, 54; Alan G. Nelson: 29, 37, 40, 53; Oxford Scientific Films: Doug Allan: 18; G.I. Bernard: 43; Stephen Dalton: 40; Alastair Shay: 12, 52; Charles Palek: 26; Robert Pearcy: 60; John L. Pontier: 8; Betty Press: 42; Leonard Lee Rue III: 8, 28, 34, 54; Michael Sacca: 23; Wilf Schurig: 50; C.W. Schwartz: 38; J.C. Stevenson: 20; Fred Whitehead: 6; Ron Willocks: 58; Harold B. Wilson: 64; Ed Wolff: 25; Leonard Zorn: 45; **Frank S. Balthis:** 4, 42; **Chicago Academy of Science:** Patrick Gulle: 5; **FPG International:** A. Schmidecker: Front Cover, 1; **International Stock Photography, Ltd.:** Mimi Cotter: 26; Keith Franklin: 57; Tom & Michele Grimm: 19, 24, 34; J. Heseltine: 15; Mike J. Howell: 10; Nena Ledbetter: 12; Maratea: 28; Steve Myers: 36; John Neubauer: 3; Dario Perla: 46; Will Regan: 28; Elliott Varner Smith: 32; J. Robert Stottlemyer: 22; Rick Strange: 30; Bill Thomas: 47; Steven C. Kaufman: 21, 32, 38, 39, 41, 46, 58; **Tom Stack & Associates:** 63; Unicorn Stock Photos: John Ebeling: 55; Dave Lyons: 4; **Vireo:** B. Chudleigh: 20; B. Henry: 30; M.P. Kahl: 33; **Rudi Von Briel:** 36; **Yogi:** R.Y. Kaufman: 9, 30, 49.

Table of Contents

Introduction

Budge

Lilac-breasted roller

Look up in the sky or peer at the branches of a tree. Listen for awhile if you are in a park or in the country. You are likely to see and hear birds. Our feathered friends can be found all over the world. They live in mountains, deserts, jungles, cities, and near oceans. They come in all colors and in many sizes. They squawk, peep, chirp, and sing. They soar and flap, dive and glide.

Birds have been on the earth for millions of years. Many people believe that birds first started out as dinosaurs. *Archaeopteryx* (ayr-kee-AYP-tuh-riks) was the first bird we know about. It was a lot like a small dinosaur. Some of the early birds grew large. Others became very small. Today there are over 9,000 different kinds of birds.

Nesting *Archaeopteryx* ▶

Life on the Wing

Osprey

Birds' bodies are made for flying. Their bones are light and hollow. Their wing muscles are large and strong.

Birds can fly because of their feathers. If you look at a feather, you will see many straight barbs growing out of the center shaft. Little hooks lock the barbs together like a zipper.

Life on the Wing

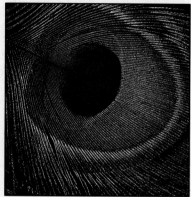

Peacock feather

Flamingo feather

When a bird flaps its wings, its flight feathers push against the air. The bird then moves up and forward. Its tail feathers help it change direction.

Birds have from 1,000 to over 25,000 feathers. Many are for flying. Other small, downy feathers next to their skin keep them warm. Once a year birds shed their feathers. This is called molting. New feathers replace the dirty, broken ones.

Scarlet macaw feather

Wild turkey feather

Molting meadowlark ▶

Tiny Fliers

Hummingbirds are amazing fliers. Their wings move so fast you can barely see them. Hummingbirds are like little helicopters. They hover in midair. They can fly up, down, sideways, and even backward.

Hummingbirds are the smallest birds. Some are only 2½ inches long. Most live in warm places. They use their long, thin bills to drink nectar, a sweet liquid in flowers.

The Peacock's Feather Fan

A bright blue bird lifts its tail and spreads its six-foot long feathers in a big fan. The markings on the ends of the feathers look like eyes. The male uses its feathers to attract a hen. The hen is brown to hide her while she sits on her eggs.

Peacocks came from Southeast Asia. Now many people keep them as pets.

Tropical Birds

Many beautiful birds live
in the tropics, which
are very warm and wet.
There are tropics in Asia,
Africa, and South America.

Parrots come in
many colors. They can
be bright green, red,
purple, blue, and yellow.

The largest parrots are
called macaws. They sit in
trees and call to each other
in their loud, harsh
voices. They use their
strong bills to crack open
hard-shelled fruits.

Tropical Birds

Bird of paradise

The fanciest birds are the birds of paradise. They have brightly colored feather fans, feather plumes along their sides, and up to three-foot-long tails.

The brightest part of a toucan (TOO-kan) is its beak. Toucan beaks can be bright yellow or green, striped with orange. The toucan uses its large and very lightweight beak to reach for fruit and berries.

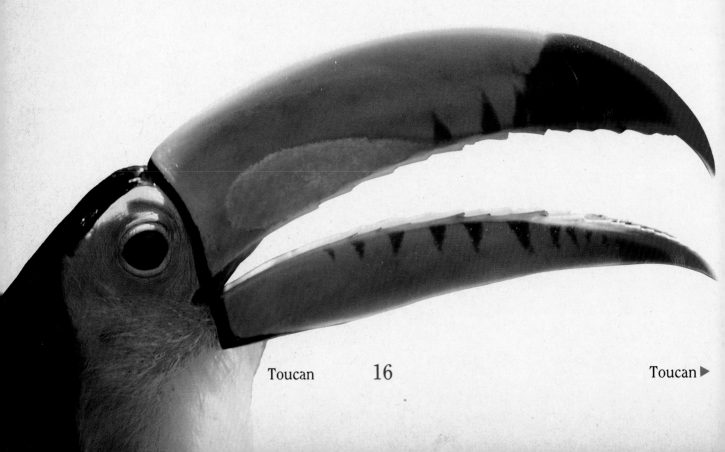

Birds That Don't Fly

Penguins

Some birds have feathers, but they can't fly. Their wings are too small. Penguins live in cold areas. Their wings are flippers that they use for swimming. They bow to each other and cackle when they meet.

Ostriches are the largest birds. They can weigh up to 300 pounds. Instead of flying, they run from enemies. They live in deserts.

Birds That Don't Fly

Emu

Roadrunners also live in the desert. Although they can fly a little, they usually run. They eat lizards, mice, and snakes. Their thick feathers protect them from snakebites.

Emus (EE-myooz) are much like ostriches. They also run quickly. An emu has long, loose feathers that almost look like hair.

Kiwis (KEE-weez) have thin, coarse feathers and no tail. They sleep during the day and hunt for food at night.

Kiwi

20

Migration

Arctic terns

Many birds can't stay warm or find food in the winter. So they fly south to warmer areas in the fall and return north in the spring. This is called migration.

Some birds migrate only a few miles. Others fly to other countries or across continents. Arctic terns travel 10,000 miles. The albatross rides the winds that circle the southern seas around the South Pole.

Tree swallows in migration ▶

Migration

Albatross

Some swallows migrate from North America to South America for the winter. In San Juan Capistrano, California, the swallows return the first day of spring. In the northeast, the honkers are a sign of spring. Honkers are Canada geese that fly in big V-shaped flocks.

No one knows how migrating birds find their way. They may follow mountains, rivers, or coastlines. Others may use the sun or stars.

Canada geese migrating ▶

Sea Gulls

Ring-billed gull

Many people think sea gulls live only by the sea. Most do, but some migrate across Texas and Oklahoma. Others travel inland to look for food.

Several kinds of gulls live on steep ocean cliffs. They build nests on little ledges. The baby birds are careful not to lean out too far. Franklin gulls float their nests in swampy marshes. As the nest sinks, the bird keeps building onto the nest.

Franklin gull nest

Sea gull

26

Special Bills for Special Diets

Mallard duck

Parrot

Birds have beaks that come in many different shapes and sizes. Each kind of bill is suited to the kinds of food a bird eats.

Birds that eat meat, fruit, or nuts have hooked beaks for tearing or cracking. Birds with long, sharp beaks spear fish or take bugs from holes in trees. The long, thin beak of the hummingbird is perfect for drinking nectar from flowers.

Baby Owl

Falcon

Hummingbird ▶

Special Bills for Special Diets

Bald eagle

Crossbill

The upper and lower parts of the crossbill's beak cross at the tips. Its beak can break apart pinecones. Birds with wide, flat beaks use them to scoop up and filter water for tasty plants.

The puffin's beak changes colors with the seasons. In the winter, it is pale and reddish. In the spring, it becomes striped with red, blue, and yellow.

Spoonbill

30

Flamingos & Pelicans

Pelican

Flamingo

Flamingos (fluh-MING-goz) and pelicans (PEL-i-kuhnz) have special beaks. Flamingos wade in shallow water on stilt legs. They move their curved beaks upside down in the water. The water runs through their beak, leaving little animals and plants.

Pelicans use their beaks like fishing nets. The bottom has a pouch that can hold up to three gallons of water. Pelicans scoop up fish as they fly.

Pelican

Flamingo ▶

Best Foot Forward

Owl talons

Falcon talons

Bird feet also come in different shapes and sizes. Birds that perch have feet that grip the perch tightly, so they don't fall off, even when they sleep. Each toe has a sharp claw. Large hunting birds have strong, big claws called talons.

A bird that walks, like the ostrich, has two toes on its foot. Wading birds have long toes and small webs. Their wide feet keep them from sinking.

Ostrich feet

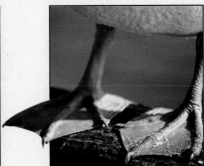

Pelican feet

Rothchild's Mynas ▶

Ducks

Ducks have paddle feet, which make them strong swimmers. They live by rivers, lakes, marshes, or along seacoasts. Most people know the "quack" sound a duck makes.

A familiar duck is the mallard. The male has a bright green head and a thin white collar of feathers around its neck. The female is brown. Her babies follow closely behind her. Sometimes they ride on her back in the water.

Hunting Birds

Bald eagle

Hunting birds have good eyesight and strong claws. Their beaks are sharp and hooked for tearing meat. They soar many miles looking for food.

The bald eagle is the national bird of the United States. Its head does not become white until it is six years old. Eagles eat mostly fish and live near rivers and lakes. Their huge nests are built in tall trees.

Red-tailed hawk

Bald eagles ▶

Hunting Birds

Hawks hunt snakes, frogs, and mice. Falcons (FAL-kuhnz) have longer wings than hawks. Peregrine (PER-uh-gruhn) falcons hunt animals on the ground and also capture small birds.

Kingfisher

Kingfishers are small hunting birds. They swoop down from a branch to catch a fish or frog in the water. Some eat reptiles and insects. Owls are night hunters. Their huge, round eyes help them see in the dark.

Peregrine falcon

40

Nest Builders

Weaverbird

Weaverbird

Weaverbird and nests

Every bird needs a nest to lay eggs in. Weaverbirds work together to bend and weave grass and straw into their nests. Each nest has a tunnel entrance.

Ovenbirds build round nests of mud. They put a small hole in the side to enter and leave. The hammerhead's nest of sticks can be several feet across and have three rooms.

Weaverbird working on nest ▶

Nest Builders

Ovenbird

Thornbill

Thornbills weave twigs into nests that look like pouches hanging from tree branches. Orioles also make hanging nests. Male bowerbirds make fancy shelters, decorated with shells, flowers, and berries, to attract a female. The female visits, then she builds her nest.

The Mallee (MAL-ee) fowl makes the biggest nest. The male builds a large mound filled with plants, where he keeps the eggs the right temperature.

Satin bowerbird

Mallee fowl on nest

Baltimore oriole ▶

Swans

A mother swan glides along the water. She bends her long neck to find plants to eat. Baby swans, called cygnets (SIG-nuhtz), follow. They're covered with grayish-white fuzz. Soon they'll have feathers. They will not be white for almost three years.

Swans live in river reeds. Their short legs make them clumsy on land. In winter, many types of swans fly south together.

Rare & Extinct Birds

Everglade kite

Some birds are rare. In the past there were many, now there are few. The Everglade kite lives in Florida. It eats snails that live in swamps. Draining the swamps has killed many snails. Now there isn't enough food for the kite.

Whooping cranes (HOO-ping KRAYNZ) survive because people help them, but they are still rare. These long-legged birds summer in Canada and winter in Texas.

Rare & Extinct Birds

Less than 60 California condors are left in North America. These huge birds have black-and-white bodies and red heads. They eat large animals that have died. A female condor lays one egg every two years. The parents care for the baby for over a year.

Thousands of passenger pigeons once filled the skies. People hunted them and cut down their forest homes. The last passenger pigeon died in 1914.

Passenger pigeon

California condor ▶

City Birds

Not all birds live in the country. Many make their homes in the city. You can see common city pigeons on window ledges of tall buildings. The ledges are like cliffs where the pigeons can sit together. Pigeons live in city parks as well.

The parks are also home to robins. These red-breasted birds listen to the ground. When they hear a worm in the ground, they grab it.

City pigeons

Robin ▶

City Birds

Purple martin

Blue jays chase hawks and owls out of parks. They like people food. They build nests out of sticks and twigs high above the ground. Purple martins are welcome city guests because they eat mosquitoes. People invite martins to live with them by putting up boxes where the birds can build their nests.

Blackbirds like city life. If there is no grass for nests, blackbirds use paper and plastic. They build their nests on building ledges.

Blackbird

Backyard Birds

Chickadee

Backyard birds are fun to watch and listen to. Chickadees look like they're wearing little black caps and gray-and-white suits. They perch on branches and sing, *"chick-a-dee-dee-dee."*

The *rat-a-tat-tat* on a tree is the sound of a woodpecker. It runs up the side of a tree, pecking for bugs. Many woodpeckers are black-and-white. Some have red crests.

Woodpecker ▶

Backyard Birds

Mockingbird

The flash of bright red might be a male cardinal. Its head feathers come to a point above its black face. Cardinals stay in one area all year long. Both males and females sing in loud, clear whistles.

The mockingbird copies the voices of many birds and animals. It can even sound like a squeaky gate or a piano. It sings many songs to chase away other birds.

58

Mockingbird

Pet Birds

Parakeet

Many birds live in houses. People enjoy listening to their pet birds sing and watching them play with bird toys.

Parakeets are the most popular pet. They are like little parrots. Some parakeets are blue and white. Others are yellow and green. They can be trained to sit on your finger or ride on your shoulder. Some parakeets can be taught to say words.

Canary ▶

Pet Birds

Zebra finch

Male canaries have sweet singing voices. The females chirp. If a canary hears music, it may try to copy it. Canaries must be covered at night so they won't sing. They also need plenty of water because they love to take baths.

Finches are happiest in pairs. Some of the most popular finches are the zebra finch, the star finch, and the red singing finch.

Star finch

Gouldian finch ▶